SHADES OF MUSIC FROM THE ECLECTIC JUKEBOX

REGGIE JOHNSON

PRELUDE

I would say music has been
a very important part of my life. Never
subjected myself to liking just one genre.
That outlook is synonymous to the way I
live life. Multi-faceted, never close-minded.
That's how I want my writing to be. And
you'll soon find out...

D N A
(Inspired by DNA, a song by Kendrick Lamar)

I got, I got, I got,
I got poetry, I got poetry inside my DNA
I used writing as a home I can go to when I need a place to stay
Prescribed this type of talent and I take it day to day

On a high, like I'm supposed to take a trip
I've been writing from a different cloth right off rip
And that way, I'm always on a wave, that's what you call
penmanship
While you try to catch a wave…
I just continue grinding, look up grinning, hit them with a smile
and wave
I got poetry, I got poetry inside my DNA
Flip through these pages and you will see the words come to life
Color in these shades of music and you will see the words in a
new light

WHY DO YOU LIKE R&B MUSIC ?

Rhythm and blues captures the emotions of writing with its melodies. As a Cancer, we are capable of tapping into our emotions more fluidly than others. R&B captures the essence of an everyday situation that you can either relate to or walk in the artist's shoes. As a writer, being able to empathize and sympathize with others has allowed me to expand my writing and let me have the courage to tell my stories.

NEW VERSUS OLD SCHOOL

Back in the days, you could listen to a song
And relate to what the singer was going through
As if you were going through it yourself
And at times I did
That love note I wanted to pass
That call or email I didn't want to receive
Times have changed
Some of the new artists do it today in their own style
The same response is not yielded equally
We live in the world of no text-backs, sliding in DMs and nudes
What happened to the days of listening to that R&B song with
the one you like?
Instead of belting out a song because you can apply it to a
situation you're currently going through
I miss those days

THE GIRLS THEY USED TO SING ABOUT

I want it to be reminiscent of the 90's
With the record player emitting behind me
The songs of love I remember hearing about
New Edition, Boyz II Men wasn't afraid to sing about
That's the same way I want to be with you
No matter the different time period
The time is love period
Declaration of love period

I want it to be reminiscent of the old R&B videos
Me dancing as I profess my love
Because if it isn't, why do I feel this way?
And why do you stay on my mind?
That's how the old song goes
That's how this new love grows
I want it to be like the girls they used to sing about, one I'm
proud to show

THE SONG I SHOULD'VE WROTE

I had everything I wanted to say to you...
But within my nature, I kept everything in
Everything bottled up that it could burst
And then you left me, and I thought you were the worst
If only I could put the words into a song
With melodies, harmonies and no worries
Then we could experience our never-ending story
Now I'm experiencing this never-ending nightmare
When I wish I could've just stayed awoke
Put all of my emotions into the song I should've wrote

NOT THE SAME LOVE SONG

I'm not going to sit here and
Say witty things and
Flash shiny things just to get you to like me
Sometimes a little chivalry goes a long way and that's quite likely
I like you and I hope you feel the same
This not the same ole love song and I hope you don't think that's
a shame
Just take my hand and come with me
I know you're scared, but it will be fine if you put your trust in
me

ODE TO H.E.R.

What I'm doing?
What I'm doing?
Pouring out all my feelings for these old girls
Pouring my insecurities for those that I gave the world
The moon and the stars and the planets if I could
Whatever she needed I had it, she knew I would
Now I'm losing
As if I had a chance
I knew I was interested in love at first glance
I knew I was entertaining love when I had my first kiss
I knew I befriended love when I danced with her in bliss
You had me like this
And you always had your way
Always...
Why couldn't you focus a little on me?
Instead of on yourself
But now, I'm just a pigment of your tainted memory with
whatever else you have left

WAKE UP ALONE
(Inspired by Wake Up Alone, a song by The Chainsmokers & Jhene Aiko)

Wake up alone...

Ain't like I'm not used to it

Love

Ain't like I'm not into it

For the free 99 plus tax cause I'm Intuit

Yeah, now I got cars, now I got clothes and now I got money

Now I got a brand and I'm try to make them all remember me

But I want to remember you

All of you

And just not as a one night stand

Not the type of person to like notes left on that night stand

Will you still be here in the morning?

When the magic is gone? Was it here all along?

Will you still care in the morning?

Do you stay when it all goes?

Or will I....?

WHY DO YOU LIKE HIP HOP MUSIC?

Hip Hop allows me to push my penmanship and develop my style of writing. Through their flow and tone I'm able to create my signature craft. Perfecting this craft is what makes doing this more rewarding.

WRITER'S DELIGHT

Let my iPhone be the cardboard box that I set up on the streets
Let the music be instrumental as my mind carries on the beat
Let my thoughts be the inner beat box as they come to fruition
Let these words be the lyrics as they were made in mint
condition
No R&B right now, this is hip hop inside of me
No need for a lawyer, there's no law abiding me
This is my writer's delight
Just some material to quench your thirst
Can't take the 90's out of me that's when I came about first
These words are meant to last but what I think comes first
You've think you've seen it all but you haven't seen the worst

NEW VERSUS OLD SCHOOL

It was all about bars
Rap battles outside where people go toe to toe
Bumping rapper's delight or the breaks from Curtis Blow
A new era...slicker than the snapback
What happened to the music where all it seems like a
bunch of clapbacks?
Diss song here and a sneak diss there
What happened to a clean beef?
Nothing in life is fair
New woes came, new flows
New adlibs and hashtag rap
New club bangers and the fresh music from the trap
We came along way but did we evolve along the way?
Some people say hip hop is dead, well it depends on the
time of day

STATUS QUO

There's enough rappers
But not enough poets
I can tell you all about it but at this point, I pretty much have to
show it
There's no need for a hook, a beat or a tempo
I just need a book, a sheet of paper and the intellect from my
temple
Hidden inside is a Legend on my Nickelodeon
No need to clean up my act, I am my own custodian
I just want to sweep the doubt from your minds
I just want to go in so you can go out of your minds
But I'm still not the status quo
Never said I was, there's a lot more for me in store

ODE TO DRAKE

Used to tell us to thank him later
But now I thank him for the inspiration
Used to think it was over, now I can see the
headlines in the making
Do right and kill everything
Fill the paper with blotches of ink
These views from Ohio are above average
than one thinks
There's more life, more life, more life
Where was you righting my wrongs instead
of fighting for what's right?
Where was you when all I had sometimes
was my iPhone and my music?
Where was you when I considered my
writings my thoughts in motion?
I want to be the one to cause quite the
commotion

LOSE YOU
(Inspired by Lose You, a song by Drake)

Same Tuesday night conversing with my psyche
Giving too much attention to whether or not
certain people like me
Giving too much attention to whether or not
they'll invite me
When I got things to see, things to do
Chess game in life, depends on the way you move
Kings move in silent, guess my name matches my
character
You too busy unlocking the next version of your
character
Like it's a character select screen
It's not what you say, it's more of what you deem
Necessary for the now, important for the later
You acting for the right now, I'm acting for the
later
My cause is a lot smaller, but my effect will be a
lot greater
So, did I lose you?

WHY DO YOU LIKE MAINSTREAM MUSIC ?

Just like in its name, mainstream music is current
and up-to-date. No matter what the situation or
tone of the song, I can adapt and tap into emotional
realms that I thought I can never experience before.

NOT YOUR AVERAGE WRITER

To not be average is a good thing
One thing that I pride on is individuality
Boxing out my creativity like I'm always playing defense
No guard up is allowed, I don't want you on the fence about me
I'm me
Aware of the rules but I make my own
No one helped me with my craft, I did this on my own
Who else you know take musical influences and style
To make my writings worthwhile?
Just to get you read them
To make it more interesting
If you're reading this, it's not too late
Thank you for letting me be great

ONE HIT WONDER

We all have that one piece
That we hope will get noticed
In any shape or form
Across any social media platform
But it's hard for writers
As we have to constantly put out more and more material
There's no such thing as a one hit wonder
Just a wonder when they going to hit it big?
Meanwhile they want to ponder how big of a hole I dig
Greater the adversity, greater the reward
Paying my debts, something none of you can afford

NOT IN IT FOR THE FAME

When I started writing down my feelings
My thoughts, my inklings
I can feel my inner woes sinking
Into the quicksand of nothingness
As I found purpose
Never how much worth my words is
Never worthless
Greater value than any money you can equate
Never leave anything up for debate
I do this for me
Not going to change the way I feel for any amount of money

RIGHT NOW

My taste buds for music depends on the flavor of
the moment
Right now, it's full of artist riding the waves of
success and dance crazes
In which people never ceases to amaze me that
where did most of the substance go?
Where did the rappers that used beat box as the
music for their flow?
Needless to say, it's not all bad, some of the
pioneers resonate here in the present
Through storytelling and different styles of
rapping artists made so effervescent
And then there's the few that can blend many
styles to become iridescent
I'm trying to take a page out of their book but I'm
still learning my lessons

ODE TO ADELE

Breaking barriers

I can send text messages for days

unlimited as my carrier

Just to say the things I want to say

Thinking it'll leave an everlasting imprint

Of your latest edition, what you consider

the real you?

I'm not reading all about it

I'm not and I won't

Just because you said hello first didn't

mean I had to have the last goodbye

Even with all of your truths all of it was

based on a lie

Now we sit faded to black and white

wishing everything was alright

Hoping someone else can be 25 for the

night

LOVE INCREDIBLE

(Inspired by Love Incredible, a song by Cashmere Cat & Camila Cabello)

I just want the feeling of you right by me
Beside me
Bonnie and Clyde, ride or die for me
And when you leave, I can't wait
Till you come back and we create
Each and everything your body missing as of late
And every time I think about you
Is just everything I want to do....

Because you make love incredible
This feeling that you got me experiencing
is insatiable
Left a mark on my heart as I found yours, that's your spot, so
indelible
You make me feel real love...
Got me wanting more

WHAT DO YOU LIKE ALTERNATIVE MUSIC ?

The genre and the meaning of the word synonymously
describes me and my taste of music very well.
Mutually exclusive, not limiting or defined. Boundless.
I like that alternative music encompass many different
styles or blends of music in order to create something
special. That's what I like to do with my writing.

AMBIENCE

Musical notes scented the room with intensity
Full of letters and majors the way college reminded me
It's everywhere and all around me
Music became what I love and now it defines me
Get exposed to the essence, don't be afraid to take a whiff
Inhale the rhythm, experience the diff

INSPIRATION

Musical notes must have been my
mattress since birth
I live and sleep for the melody
The instrumentation
The lyrics
The simple anatomy of music
envelopes from the core
Having an ear for this music is a
blessing that many people enjoy
That's my joy and no one can tell me
otherwise

MOTIVATION

I could say it a hundred times before the
words can leave an imprint
Nothing taken seriously until they see it
in print
Well I have 5 books now and the
blessings have come ever since
music, family and love, everlasting
permanence
Plus or minus a few, no additions could
make a difference
Sometimes the math doesn't make sense
When it all else fails, leave it to the
writing for everything to make sense

DEDICATION

I want to be the poetic Weezy
A la the Dedication mixtapes
Embrace the diligence instead of
capitalizing on my mistakes
Stay direct on my shots instead of
focusing on my missed takes
Living in this world like it's a movie
Because people flip the script acting as if
they all trustworthy
Just trust me...
When I say, this is not only a pastime
I'm dedicated to the pen, more than a
lyric more than a rhyme

IT WON'T KILL YA
(Inspired by It Won't Kill Ya, a song by The Chainsmokers & Louane)

You stay entertaining the...
Idea of us becoming we...
But I sense insecurities...
That makes time begin to freeze
And you always be so cold
Why couldn't you follow heart and do as
your told?
Because I keep telling myself I'll wait for
you
I keep telling myself to save the date for
you
I want you tell me "I think I'm late...for
you"
Talk to me...it won't kill ya

WHAT DO YOU LIKE ABOUT REGGAE MUSIC?

Fluidity. Music in motion. Reggae music has always
been the genre to make people move, make me
people dance. Make people feel something. That's
what I aim to do with my writing sometimes.

RHYTHM

Rectifying old memories of
How we would move to
Your heartbeat and mine
That I shed a tear
How we didn't save that last dance and
Most of all, that I left you on the dance floor

FLUIDITY

Effortlessly…
You left me speechless
The way you whine your body on me
Immersed in the movement that I don't
want to come up for air
The way you pick it up slow and bring
back down there
And you do it with a smile on your face
The smile of a woman, best feeling that
can't be replaced

SEXUAL

I wish I had her number
Or better remember it for the sake of
this time of night
That calling in the night time for that
late-night hookup
Whenever we come together, a flame
of passion ignites, that can burn any
bedroom down
It all started when we were dancing
Winding it up pon de riddim
As lifeless as we end up, you can see
how we are living
And then she goes home, until the next
time she calls
When she begins to dutty wine, all of my
worries begin to fall

IN SYNC

No letting go and no holding back
Because I Wayne Wonder sometimes if
we remain in sync
Not saying bye bye bye and before it you
know, you're long gone
These ain't the time for early 2000 teen
songs
These are the times for us to be picking
theme songs
These are the times that you could be
righting my wrongs
And I could be down on one knee
And you could be saying I do
On my Ray Charles, I'm a make it do
what it do

ODE TO SEAN PAUL

I'm still in love...
With you or with the music I'm not really
sure
Because both reactions strike a nerve down
in my core
The infatuation increases, got me wanting
more
So gimme the light and watch the freaks
come out in the dark
So up with it girl, bounce with it girl
Do it how you want, I'm in your world
Don't stop moving, keep on dancing
Love comes with a coat, no freelancing

WHAT IS THE SIGNIFIANCE OF A JUKEBOX?

I remember these from my childhood
and I always had a fascination with them.
The ability to house all of these different
genres of music at one's disposal. That's
how I envision the makeup of my mind.
Any rhythm, beat or tempo that strikes my
ear that I like, no matter what genre, is
something I take pride in. Broadening my
scope has allowed me to appreciate and
reach more realms of music by listening to
many different styles.

LOYALTY
(Inspired by Loyalty, a song by Kendrick Lamar & Rihanna)

Loyalty, loyalty, loyalty
Tell me who you loyal to
Don't be board gaming me
Thinking that you trustworthy and I
ain't have a clue
No blue paw print, didn't have a clue
No Nick Jr over here, we the squad
Minimize our credit check, cause we
ain't dealing with no frauds
You over putting on a show thinking
it yields an applaud
It's so hard to be humble yet it's not
hard for me to be honest
Check your own self before you
claiming someone dishonest

HONEST
(Inspired by Honest, a song by The Chainsmokers)

Sitting here thinking...

Where did I go wrong with you?

As a lover?

As a friend?

When this was beginning, I didn't think it would end

Never by any means did I mean that you were a

means to an end

Never did anything shallow, so how did we go off the

deep end

How did our love become the topic of a trend?

Guess we weren't social enough

Communicating our issues

Are you gonna need some tissues?

My heart already cried enough over you

Now I'm already over you

I just need closure

My heart needs a new home, not a foreclosure

And I'm just being honest

COME OVER
(Inspired by Come Over, a song by Trey Songz

Some say shyness is a sign of weakness
But with you as my highness, my
intentions are the sincerest
The queen you are fit for a king, since it's
all in my name
No need for rules, I ensure I ain't playing
no games
Seeing the differences in each other shows
we are one in the same
We complement each other
I like to make you feel good so I
compliment her more than others
So can I say won't you come over
And once we start this thing, there are no
do overs

CAN'T HAVE EVERYTHING
(Inspired by Can't Have Everything, a song by Drake)

Aw man
This is everything
Really everything
Married to the pen, where's my wedding ring
Walking down the aisle, let the people sing

And we gathered here today
I'm a writer first and I have something to say
I do this from time to time not worrying about a dime
If you stuck in the past, well you gonna have to do your time

Can't have everything
But I won't settle for nothing less
First up so I'm not settling for second best
I want to be the only answer not taking a second guess
I'm never gonna get tired, so you don't need to hear the rest

BOO'D UP
(Inspired by Boo'd Up, a song by Ella Mai)

Feelings

Got me caught in some feelings

Don't know what's happening

You think it's flattering

That I'm all in my feelings

But I don't know what to say

What words to mutter for you but be that

as it may

Never experienced any of this before you

Trying to solve the mystery on my own

when I don't have a clue

Guess you're the ish Sherlock

The way you got me on lock

Times running down and got you on the

clock

REGRET IN YOUR TEARS
(Inspired by Regret In Your Tears, a song by Nicki Minaj)

Crying ashes from your eyelashes
just to show you how bad your
burned me
A frown becomes a smirk just the
same as how you turned on me
And still you had me twisted over
you, on my Keith Sweat
Paying for all your wrongdoings
and now I'm in debt
Are you gonna give me back my
heart?
Are you gonna put it back
together after you ripped it apart?
Are we gonna finish this thing
after we let it start?

I DON'T KNOW WHY
(Inspired by I Don't Know, a song by STAR Cast)

When we first hung out...
Started out just friends
Too laced up, trying to tie up loose ends
I didn't know if it was good for us or knot
I just know that I felt something when I'm
with you and it was greater when I'm not
Then you went away
I didn't know what to say
And I still get to talk to you from time to
time and day to day
Didn't think I was good enough
But at that time I was just mad
But I get the chance to say somethings and
I'm glad
I don't know why I stopped crushing on you
It was hard to move on from you
But I see it's still something there
And everything is not fair
And I just want you be there

ESCAPE
(Inspired by Escape, a song by Kehlani)

Never really thought I could do it

Never really thought I'd be this scared

Never would've said it out loud

And so you would've never been aware

I don't want you thinking of me any differently

And I don't want you be any less to me

All I want is to have more

Even though we don't always see eye to eye,
your heart is what

I still adoreCounting down the moments until
you become what

I live for

Even though I can't make you lose yourself
looking for me

And I can't let you make me your everything

All I wanna be is an escape

Just let me be an escape

Maybe sometime we escape

Escape

SLIP & FALL
(Inspired by Slip & Fall, a song by Elhae and Eric Bellinger)

Free from innocence
bask in the effervescent bliss
I'm here to shoot my shot, hope I don't miss
Sometimes I pass on opportunities, so I can
get the assists
So can you assist me here...
In this bed...
Could you think of other things we can do
instead?
I can think of many things I can only do with
your legs
Drunk on love and your body is the keg and
tonight I'm going to slip and fall
and when it happens don't pick me up
fallen for your love and don't make me get up

HOW DID YOU COME UP WITH THE TITLE?

I wanted something to encompass the core being of who I am past, present and future. Music has always been multifaceted and that describes me to a T. Each genre helps shed a new layer and develops me on an emotional, intellectual, and physical layer. I remember having a jukebox in my parent's basement that would hold all of these vinyls in a carousel. I always used to think that was one of the coolest things as a child. When I think of how music has played an important part of my life. I think of that from my childhood. That is how I came up with Shades of Music from the Eclectic Jukebox.

IN SYNC

Maybe you weren't ready...
Maybe you thought I was CRZY...
Yeah, at first you thought it was a distraction
From your normal day to day
Trying out this poetry thing
And then you start doing this undercover
Even keeping it from me and that was doing too much
Then, all of sudden you went from being underground to
mainstream
You were 2 On
So, I'm like can we pretend
That everything was like yesterday
You were just the one that in your feelings
How many times did I have to say, get them out and you'll
make a killing?
Then you went all hands on deck, when you had that one good
performance
Had to work for it and cease the moment
I guess I changed your life and that's all fine and dandy
Now you expect the finer things thinking you living all fancy
I just don't want you to get caught up in the fantasy
And I don't want you choking on your words when listening to
what I have to say
I want you to be something bigger than a Kehlani, Iggy or a
Tinashe

PUBLISHING

9 781545 428603